ELECTILE
DYSFUNCTION

An Adult Comedy Coloring Book

ELECTILE DYSFUNCTION

Charlie Hall

Willow Street Press New York

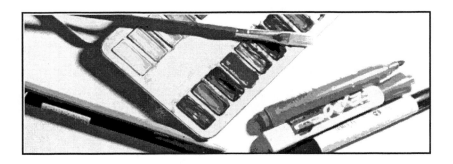

DIRECTIONS

Option 1

Open book. Find page. Read poem and laugh. Apply color to drawing, trying to stay in the lines. Go right over the gray areas. For the medium, something translucent- like watercolors, water-color pencils, or markers are best but colored pencils, pastels, and the like are adequate too. Stay away from spray paint.

Option 2

Follow all the directions of option 1 except for anything pertaining to art, art supplies or coloring. Relax, laugh, enjoy.

Introduction

Coloring books for the adults
Boast how they lower stress.
But humor also does the trick
Perhaps with more success.

So intricate are some books
It seems more like work than art.
With ours though, there's no pressure
Either color it, or not!

We're sure you'll bust a gut
At our "colorful" depiction
Until you realize
This book's sold in non-fiction!

WARNING!

For dysfunctioning elections
Laughing hard can help remission
But laugh hard past 4 hours?
Please seek a trained physician.

2012 – Obama wins
It's more than Mitt can bear.
"I'm just another John McCain
With height and better hair."

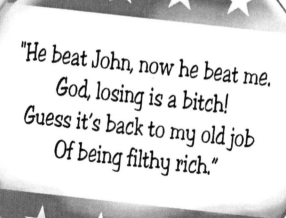

"He beat John, now he beat me.
God, losing is a bitch!
Guess it's back to my old job
Of being filthy rich."

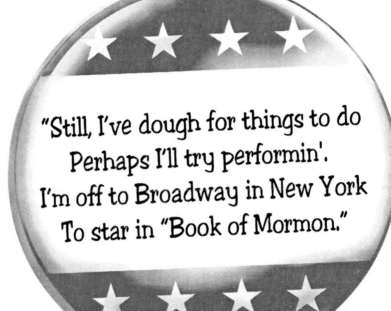

"Still, I've dough for things to do
Perhaps I'll try performin'.
I'm off to Broadway in New York
To star in "Book of Mormon.""

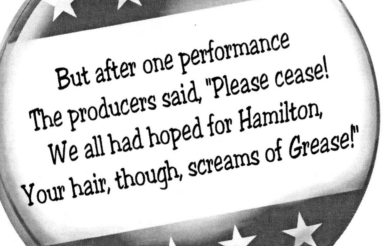

But after one performance
The producers said, "Please cease!
We all had hoped for Hamilton,
Your hair, though, screams of Grease!"

Swiftly did four years pass by
New elections were in view.
Who would run for president?
Which states were red, which blue?

"Too bad they're all not purple!"
a famed dinosaur would shout.
"Be careful what you wish for,"
Said his friend who had come out.

The GOP, with Romney out,
Searched for someone new.
"Candidates don't grow on trees –
We might find one or two."

Well, two dozen swaggered in.
"We'll beat that Clinton chick!
What's she got that we don't?"
One joked, "a bigger...demographic."

The list was Kasich, Cruz, and Jeb
Plus Jindal, Christie, Perry.
Add Rubio, Pataki - hey,
Was Rand Paul necessary?

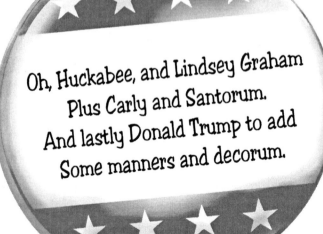

Oh, Huckabee, and Lindsey Graham
Plus Carly and Santorum.
And lastly Donald Trump to add
Some manners and decorum.

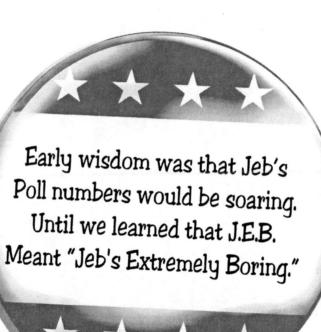

Early wisdom was that Jeb's
Poll numbers would be soaring.
Until we learned that J.E.B.
Meant "Jeb's Extremely Boring."

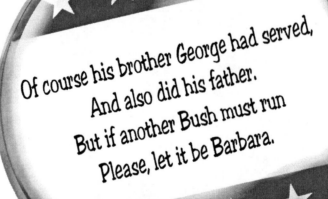

Of course his brother George had served,
And also did his father.
But if another Bush must run
Please, let it be Barbara.

Ben Carson showed great brilliance
For months he led the pack.
A surgeon, an outsider,
A Republican.....and black!

"Ben proves we are diverse now,"
His Grand Old Party stressed.
"Too bad he's not transgendered –
He'd have triple the success!"

Often Ben would close his eyes.
"It's just the way I think."
"Or", said Trump, "the Ambien
I slipped into your drink."

Now covering this race for us,
The newsies from TV,
Who meet to drink and gossip
And make fun of BBC.

George says "Let's play poker!"
The others slur, "Why not!"
No one knows who's winning
'Cept for Chuck Todd and his chart.

CNN is buying drinks
For MSNBC
And Fox News at the bar drinks scotch
Poured – get this – liberally!

Matt has only one merlot.
"I won't become, you see,
A sloppy, soggy wino –
Hey, where's Hoda & Kathie Lee?"

Soon Blitzer said I'm leaving,
Then Rachel, Rush, and Lauer.
Then the 60 Minutes team
Who always stay one hour.

The Christian right adored Ted Cruz:
"He's a perfect fit."
His colleagues partially agreed:
"He's a perfect dick."

Nicknames like "a wacko bird"
And "Toxic Ted" were vented
John Boehner called him Lucifer
Which Lucifer resented.

Trump nicknamed him "Lying Ted"
Causing sides to split.
His next was "Crooked Hillary"
Showing his great wit.

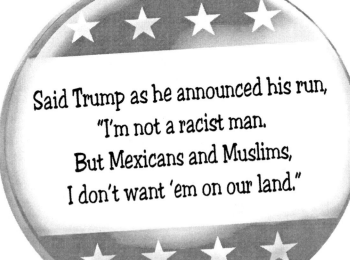

Said Trump as he announced his run,
"I'm not a racist man.
But Mexicans and Muslims,
I don't want 'em on our land."

"We're going to build a wall" he said,
"And what we'll pay is none.
Believe me when I say this:
If I build it, they won't come."

We interrupt this poem for a new nursery rhyme...

Humpty Trumpty
built a "yuuuge" wall
To keep out the Mexicans
once and for all.

"You have no more jobs here,
so please don't uproot.
Our National Guard
will now pick
our fruit!"

Trumpty continued,
"Way back in the day
We shoulda built one
barring Canada, eh?

Celine and pro hockey
would sadly be gone
But a wall might've
kept Ted Cruz where
he was born."

"And speaking of that,
Marco Rubio, too,
Was born down in Cuba,
I hear might be true.

Now as for my birth,
it has never been shady
Everyone knows that
I'm Rosemary's
Baby."

We now return to your regulary scheduled poem already in progress.

John Kasich from Ohio struck
A very different tone.
He was positive, and upbeat
Very hopeful, but unknown.

To prove his optimism
Was sincere and not just bull,
He'd fill glasses to half empty
But would call them each "half full."

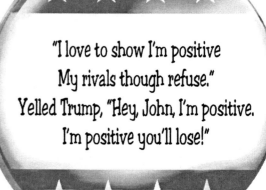

"I love to show I'm positive
My rivals though refuse."
Yelled Trump, "Hey, John, I'm positive.
I'm positive you'll lose!"

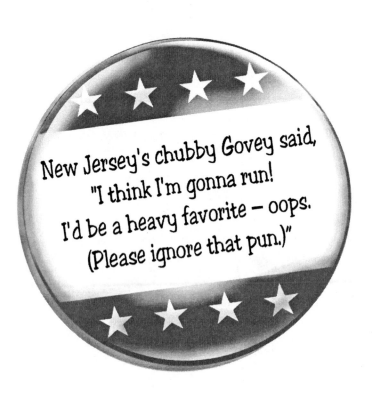

New Jersey's chubby Govey said,
"I think I'm gonna run!
I'd be a heavy favorite — oops.
(Please ignore that pun.)"

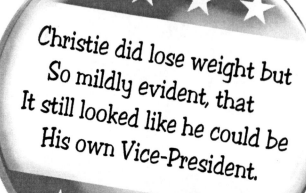

Christie did lose weight but
So mildly evident, that
It still looked like he could be
His own Vice-President.

Rubio was smart, and brash,
Rehearsed, at times neurotic –
Repeating talking points so much
He struck folks as robotic.

Now Disneyworld's in Florida
Where Marco makes his home.
And Disney uses robots for
Attractions, it's well known.

So in that Hall of Presidents,
If Abe or George don't run,
Marco could fill in...
It's as close as he might come.

For the televised debates,
The hoard of hopefuls split.
Half were chosen for prime time
The others felt like...number 2.

Low blows turned debates low brow
From insults they would make –
As good as TV wrestling
Except this wasn't fake.

Now on to the Democrats
And Clinton's race to lose
Against four no-name white guys
This soiree would be a snooze.

Aside from Bernie Sanders,
On the ballot was Jim Webb,
Gov'nors Mart O'Malley,
And Linc Chafee -well 'nuf said.

Some shared ideas worth noting
While others caused a yawn
Linc offered, "let's go metric!"
And poof! Next day was gone.

Now closing in on Hillary
Unphased and nonchalant
Was pesky Bernie Sanders
A curmudgeon from Vermont.

Now if you don't know Bernie
Try to pick out carefully
The puppet, and the cartoon,
And the one with OCD.

WHERE'S ~~WALDO~~ BERNIE?

At Sanders' college rallies
The crowd would loudly cheer
At thoughts of free tuition
(Giving them more dough for beer).

Yes Bernie felt their anger,
Felt their fear, and their concern
And once in a reversal
One supporter "felt the Bern!"

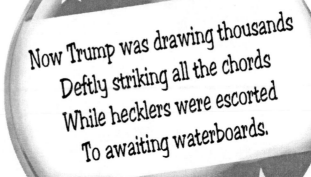

Now Trump was drawing thousands
Deftly striking all the chords
While hecklers were escorted
To awaiting waterboards.

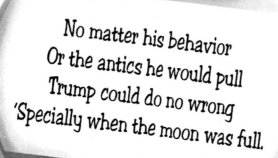

No matter his behavior
Or the antics he would pull
Trump could do no wrong
'Specially when the moon was full.

On to the first 2 primaries
To see who'd pass the test –
Bernie, Carly, Teddy?
Some votes for Kanye West?

In Iowa they 'caucus'
Freely sharing what they think
While others think that 'cauc' is
Used when you install a sink.

New Hampshire, next, so vital
Though many wonder why
When voters there can't choose
If they should live free, or should die.

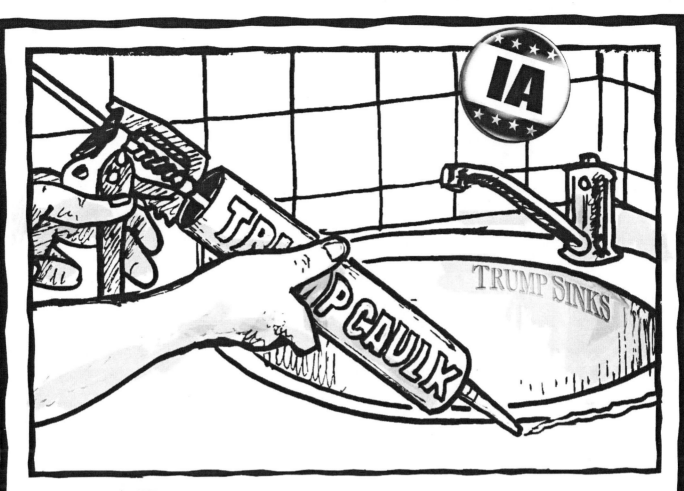

Cruz would win in Iowa
Leaving Trump behind
And Hillary claimed victory
As Bernie yelled, "We tied!"

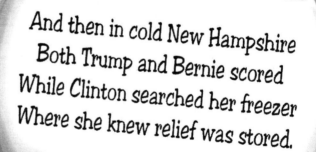

And then in cold New Hampshire
Both Trump and Bernie scored
While Clinton searched her freezer
Where she knew relief was stored.

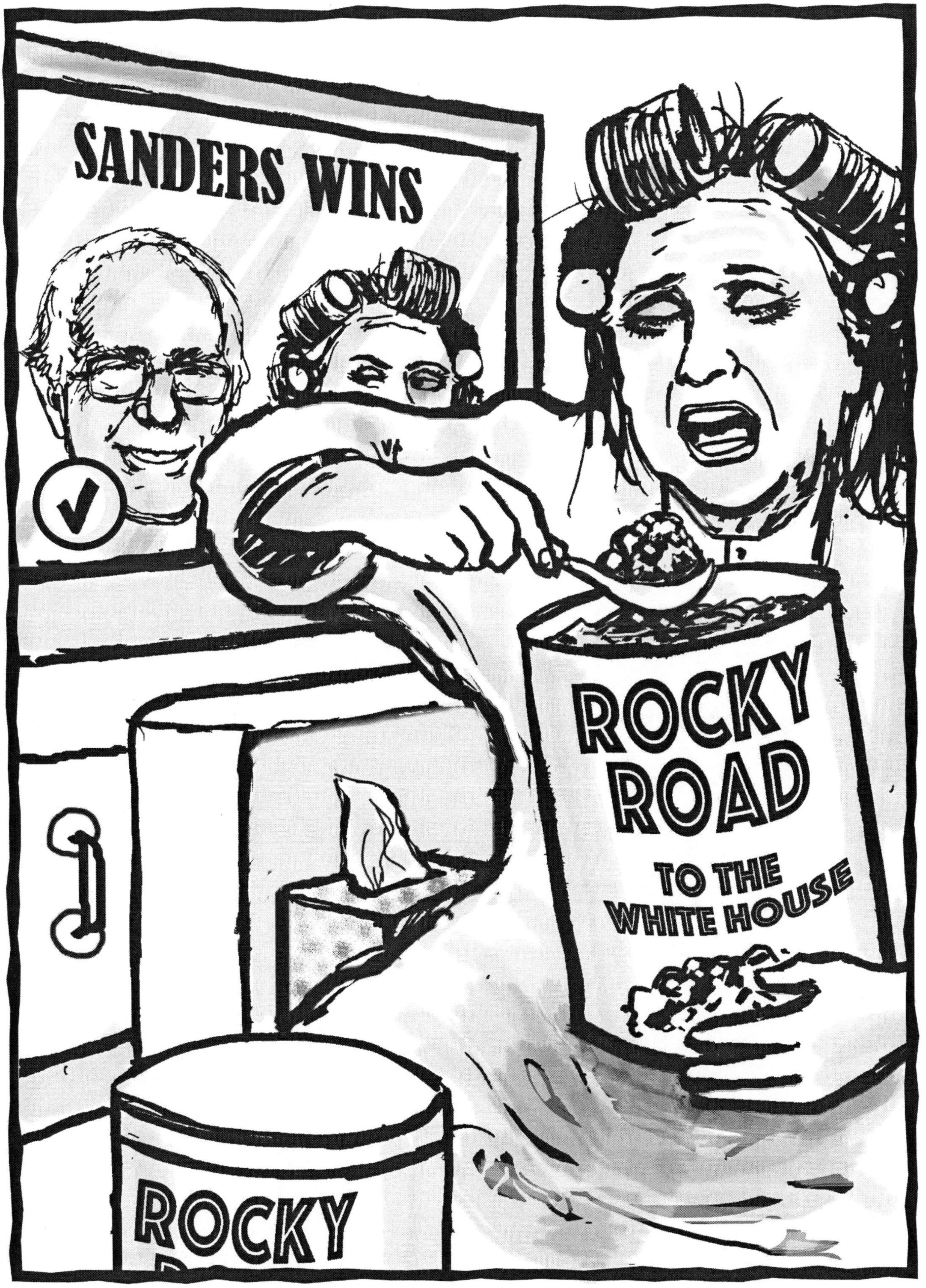
SANDERS WINS
ROCKY ROAD
TO THE WHITE HOUSE
ROCKY

And we interrupt again so we may <u>reflect</u> on this fairy tale rhyme…

Mirror mirror
Hear my plea
Someone's disrespected me.
"That face," remarked this malcontent,
"Imagine it as president!"
This ill-coiffed cad will so atone
For saying this in *Rolling Stone.*

Carly, yes
I saw it there
From that ass with orange hair.
There's a spell I can install that
Makes his hands shrink very small.
And if you want, besides the hands
I'll shrink one of his favorite glands!

Thank you mirror,
That'd be great
But rumor is
You'd be too late!
(LOL)

We now return to your regularly scheduled poem already in progress.

When Bernie met the Pope
How his reputation swelled
Though students were more wowed
That he appeared on SNL.

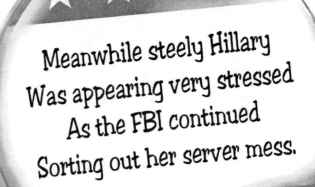

Meanwhile steely Hillary
Was appearing very stressed
As the FBI continued
Sorting out her server mess.

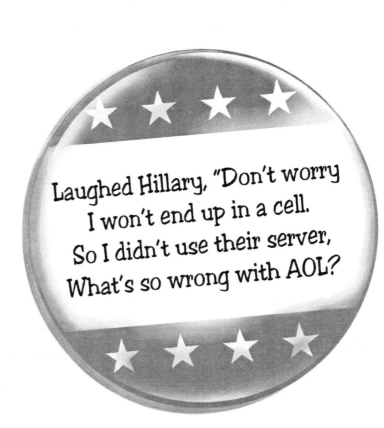

Laughed Hillary, "Don't worry
I won't end up in a cell.
So I didn't use their server,
What's so wrong with AOL?

"Nuthin'," said her husband
Working crowds so charmingly.
The people always loved him
Oh, and one quite literally.

The Fox debate caused trouble
Megyn's questions were decried.
Trump pleaded, "Where's my softballs?"
Megyn said, "Behind your fly."

While Trump made his thoughts clearer
Megyn pondered his hygiene.
"They make Trump Steaks, Trump Neckties,
They should make Trump Listerine."

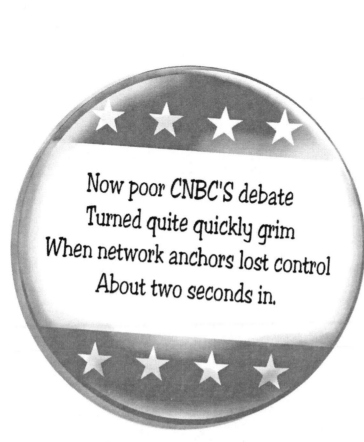

Now poor CNBC'S debate
Turned quite quickly grim
When network anchors lost control
About two seconds in.

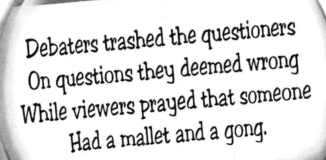

Debaters trashed the questioners
On questions they deemed wrong
While viewers prayed that someone
Had a mallet and a gong.

Then a tragic situation
Judge Scalia passed one day.
Republicans barked: "Don't you dare
Replace him 'til we say!"

Obama said, "Hey, that's our job
To find a judge, you see?
And this choice was obvious:
Judge Judy, from TV!"

The other judges had their doubts,
"Her fine show we've all witnessed.
But there is just one small concern
Judge Judy scares us s#!tless!"

At a Clinton rally
Mad'line Albright was heard tell,
"For women who don't help women
There's a special place in hell!"

Some ladies there were livid
Some said, "She has some gall!"
And some found that Ms. Albright
Wasn't really bright at all.

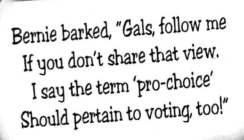

Bernie barked, "Gals, follow me
If you don't share that view.
I say the term 'pro-choice'
Should pertain to voting, too!"

Marco just to needle Trump
Quipped, "Boy, your hands are small."
Trump replied, "I don't talk size
With Cubans 4 feet tall."

"Besides, the T-Rex had small hands
And they were vicious beasts.
Mostly 'cause their happy place
Their arms could never reach

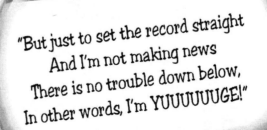

"But just to set the record straight
And I'm not making news
There is no trouble down below,
In other words, I'm YUUUUUUGE!"

Of the top tier, Christie
Was the first to end his run.
Endorsing Trump who told him
"Stand behind me and look dumb."

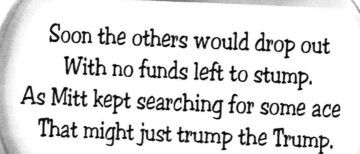

Soon the others would drop out
With no funds left to stump.
As Mitt kept searching for some ace
That might just trump the Trump.

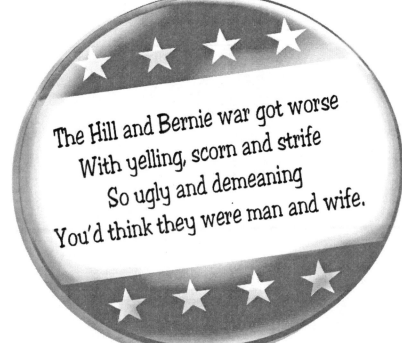

The Hill and Bernie war got worse
With yelling, scorn and strife
So ugly and demeaning
You'd think they were man and wife.

"She's got those SUPER delegates,"
As Bernie's anger grew.
"A shame this isn't Seinfeld,
I'd yell, 'no more sup-er for you!'"

John Kasich kept campaigning
Implying through his words,
"If Trump and Cruz both falter,
I'll swoop in for sloppy thirds."

Would Kasich be a footnote?
Would they drink to him at bars?
Or was he now a loser
Doomed for *Dancing with the Stars*?

Said Trump, "I need a VP now
Who's brash, and mean and loud
Assertive, yet well-cultured,
Hey is picking ME allowed?

John McCain's pick for VP
Still haunts him to this day.
"If I knew then, what I know now
I'd have gone with Tina Fey."

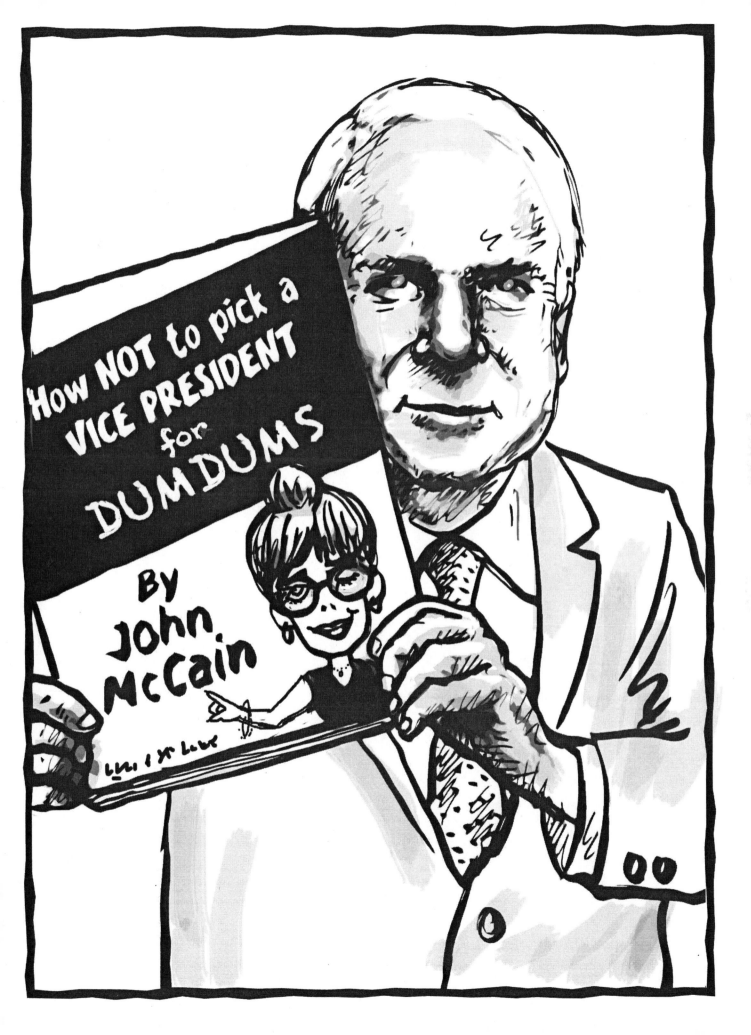

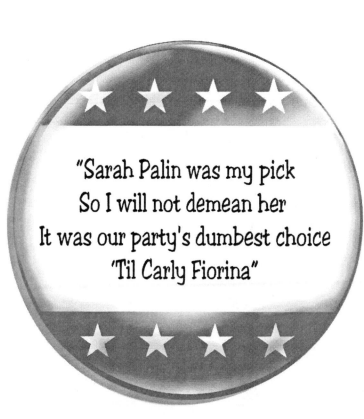

"Sarah Palin was my pick
So I will not demean her
It was our party's dumbest choice
'Til Carly Fiorina"

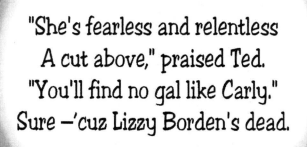

"She's fearless and relentless
A cut above," praised Ted.
"You'll find no gal like Carly."
Sure —'cuz Lizzy Borden's dead.

The Clinton/FBI report
Showed just how lax she'd been.
Routinely she poo-pooed it,
"I'll pardon myself when I win."

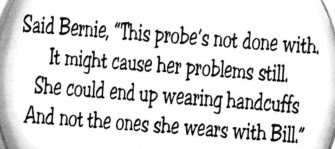

Said Bernie, "This probe's not done with.
It might cause her problems still.
She could end up wearing handcuffs
And not the ones she wears with Bill."

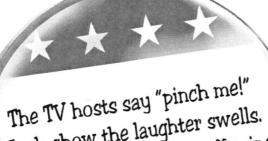
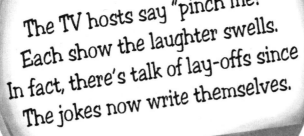

The TV hosts say "pinch me!"
Each show the laughter swells.
In fact, there's talk of lay-offs since
The jokes now write themselves.

Yes Conan, Trevor, Ellen,
Plus Steve and Seth, I hear
Are begging, with the Jimmys
For elections every year.

Why not? It's just like sex
When election punch lines kill.
To them it's quite orgasmic
and Trump is their blue pill.

Ol' Bern felt like a kid again
And showed no signs of slowing,
Much like that pink bunny
He kept going and going and going...

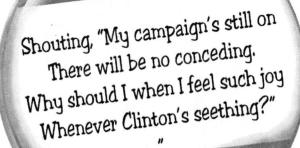

Shouting, "My campaign's still on
There will be no conceding.
Why should I when I feel such joy
Whenever Clinton's seething?"
"

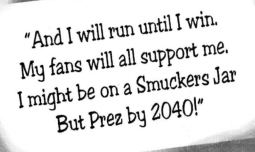

"And I will run until I win.
My fans will all support me.
I might be on a Smuckers Jar
But Prez by 2040!"

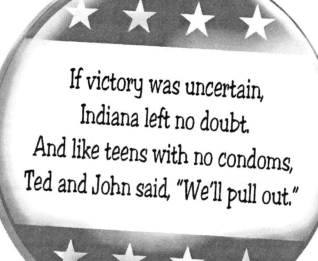

If victory was uncertain,
Indiana left no doubt.
And like teens with no condoms,
Ted and John said, "We'll pull out."

With Trump presumptive nominee
Republicans felt dizzy.
"Our party chose a reality star?
What, Richard Hatch too busy?"

NATIONAL NOOSE
AMERICAS MOST UNRELIABLE NEWS SOURCE
SEE DICK RUN!
Survivor Richard Hatch replaces Trump
Wants more transparency, less penal codes
GOP: JUST TRADING ONE FOR ANOTHER
WEINER
Grabbed For VP
TRUMP MOVING TO MEXICO

Now we would be remiss
If we do not remark
On Trumpster's famous "do"
Or the toupee-that-is-not.

Its growth has more directions
Than a dresser from IKEA.
But that's not all so bad...
When your head's gone
CH-CH-CHIA!

Yes, ChiaTrump's in stores now
And so not to get lonely
They made a ChiaClinton
That gets slammed by
ChiaComey.

The FBI said, "There's no crime."
Perhaps a wise decision
Or we could need an Oval Cell
Inside some federal prison.

EGO
NOT
INCLUDED

ChiaTRUMP

JUST ADD
WATER
FROM FLINT, MI.

CHIA WALL
SOLD
SEPARATELY

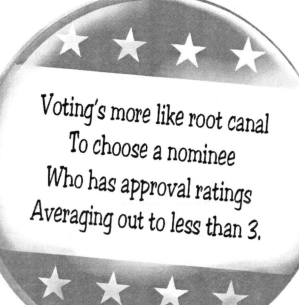

Voting's more like root canal
To choose a nominee
Who has approval ratings
Averaging out to less than 3.

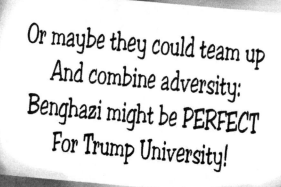

Or maybe they could team up
And combine adversity:
Benghazi might be PERFECT
For Trump University!

The lesser of two weasels?
Flip a coin, and make a call?
Vote Green or Libertarian?
Move up to Montreal?

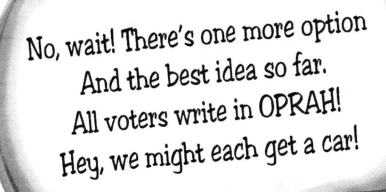

No, wait! There's one more option
And the best idea so far.
All voters write in OPRAH!
Hey, we might each get a car!

Be a celebrity! Draw, trace, or glue in a picture of yourself (or a friend) right in between our stars for a custom coloring book. Be creative. Use the blank buttons above for your own poem, or prose. Makes a great gift!

Alas it's time we take our leave
We're down to final pages.
If you found the past a hoot
The future looks outrageous!

Breaking at this point in time
Was always our intention.
How else could we sell these
Trendy books at each convention?

So no applause – it's time to pause
Don't fret, we'll have resumption
With a sequel even more
Electile-y dysfunctioned.

EPILOGUE

Will Trump release his taxes?
Revealing his true worth?
Will Christie lose his pants belt?
Revealing his true girth?

Will Hillary's new server
Be rigged with an alarm?
And will we hear it blaring
When Bill's on match.com?

Do we ban all Muslims?
Or will they stay away
Due to endless airport lines
Caused by the TSA?

Will Trump soon be accepted
by Grand Old Party peers?
Will Melania's next speech start with
"Four score and seven years..."

And these are just a few
Of the queries on our mind
That will give our coming sequel
Many reasons for a rhyme.

- Charlie Hall

ABOUT THE AUTHOR

Charlie Hall is an artist and comedian from Providence, RI. He graduated from the Rhode Island School of Design in 1978 and promptly became a stand-up comic for 30 years, much to the delight of his financially-drained parents.

Years of honing his craft led to appearances on national TV shows such as Star Search and the Joan Rivers Show, and he has opened for scores of headlining acts including Frankie Valli, Chicago, Kool & the Gang, Sam Kinison, Reba McEntire, and Jerry Seinfeld. Charlie is an award-winning political cartoonist, TV news courtroom artist, theater producer, art teacher, illustrator and caricaturist. He also penned the lyrics for the official state song of Rhode Island.

Feel free to contact Charlie at charliehall@cox.net.

ACKNOWLEDGMENTS

This book would not have seen the light of day without artist/buddy Lucas Kolasa who suggested I create it, comic Tom Cotter who hooked me up with his publisher Willow Street Press, and Susan Konig, boss lady of said company. Also big thanks to the talented Jake Gorke, along with two great friends: collaborator David Rampone, and vulture capitalist Chris Harris both of whom provided generous, much needed, much appreciated support. Yes, I said vulture. Props to Jane, Liza, Sonic, Doreen, Dave, Tom, Gil, the Twins, and Jerry's Artarama. And lastly deep, heartfelt thanks, love and appreciation to Hillary Clinton and Donald Trump. Couldn't have done it without you.